uit of the sea... y
broil it, bake it, sauté it.
s, shrimp creole, shrimp
, pan-fried shrimp, deep-
rimp, peel'n'eat shrimp,
p with fried rice, shrimp
aked shrimp, barbecued
p, shrimp butter, shrimp
er, coconut fried shrimp,
imp, shrimp étouffée,..

"Our house had been in Mama's family since her grandpa's grandpa's grandpa came across the ocean about a thousand years ago, or somethin' like that."

Mama Blue's Steamed Shrimp, page 8

THE BUBBA GUMP SHRIMP CO.
COOKBOOK

This is a Time Inc. Ventures Custom Publishing Book.

Recipes and food photography
©1994 Oxmoor House, Inc.
Box 2463, Birmingham, AL 35201

FORREST GUMP script and photography
©1994 Paramount Pictures. All Rights Reserved.
Oxmoor House Authorized User.

Foreword ©1994 Winston Groom

All rights reserved. No part of this book may be reproduced in any form or by any means without the prior written permission of the publisher, excepting brief quotes in connection with reviews written specifically for inclusion in a magazine or newspaper.

Library of Congress Catalog Card Number: 94-68590
ISBN: 0-8487-1479-2

Printed in the U.S.A.
First Printing 1994

Cover inset photo: *Jenny's Southwestern Shrimp,* page 31

To order more copies of THE BUBBA GUMP SHRIMP CO. COOKBOOK, write to Oxmoor House, P.O. Box 2463, Birmingham, AL 35201

Contents

7	foreword
11	you can bake it
27	you can barbecue it
33	you can boil it
69	you can fry it
79	you can sauté it
101	goes real good with

Dedicated to the memory of
Benjamin Buford "Bubba" Blue

Bubba and me were partners for life.

Dear Cooks,

    As most of you know, I've done a lot of stuff in my time — and some of it waddun so easy. But I'm havin' a real good time now, 'cause me and Li'l Forrest, we're buddies. Bein' a daddy comes real natural to me. Sorta like a duck in water, whatever that means.

    What me and Li'l Forrest like to do best is cook in the kitchen. And cookin' shrimp is the best. All kinds of shrimp: brown shrimp, white shrimp, red shrimp, gray bay shrimp. And I'm writin' down all the recipes so's Li'l Forrest will have 'em for the whole rest of his life.

    My mama used to always say that the best place to get your shrimp recipes is from *Southern Livin'* magazine. And that's what she did, so I'm sharin' some of her favorite ones with you. Mama would've liked that.

    You don't have to be rich, famous, or even smart to cook shrimp. I'm livin' proof of that.

    Guess we like cookin' shrimp best 'cause of Ol' Bubba. I sure miss Bubba. We was friends for life.

    Bubba taught me everything there is in the shrimpin' business. Everything about catchin' 'em, cookin' 'em, and eatin' 'em — even used to tell me about pickin' up shrimps when he was a boy and ticklin' their feelers to make 'em wiggle. When me and Bubba were in the army, 'most everything he talked about eventually got back to shrimp. I'd say, "Bubba, will you help me shine my shoes?" He'd say, "Heck Forrest, I can put a shine on them shoes like the shine on a Royal Red Shrimp." Stuff like that. Anyway, Bubba got himself killed in Vietnam. And that's all I got to say about that.

The shrimpin' business was real kind to me and Bubba. I just wanted to catch enough shrimp to make a livin' and have a few left over for ourselves. But me and Lieutenant Dan… well, we got pretty lucky. And even tho' Ol' Bubba's gone now, since we was partners for life, I gave Bubba's mama his share. She's livin' real good now.

Anyways, Mama Blue taught me the best way to make shrimp there ever was. Mama Blue had good and simple ways of doing things. And simple is something I can understand. Anyhow, I want to tell you this recipe of hers now, so's you can do it yourself.

Mama Blue's Steamed Shrimp

First, get a big old iron pot with a lid on it. (Mama Blue called hers a "scaldron.")

Next, get about two or three pounds of them real big shrimp — them they call "jumbos." They're about 10 to 12 of 'em to the pound, and they'll serve six to eight people (unless it's me!). Almost look like lobsters! (Heads on or off, it don't matter.)

Next, cut off three or four onion tops and the green tops off a celery stalk.

Then open a can of cheap beer. Drink half the beer. (Mama Blue liked this part.)

Get the scaldron going real hot on the stove. Then throw in the onions and celery tops till they start to wilt. When the stuff begins to make a funny hissin' sound, pour in half the beer you ain't drank yet.

When the beer begins to steam and bubble up good, throw in the shrimp. Put the lid on the pot good and tight, and wait about four minutes.

Open the lid. Shrimp ought to be turnin' a little pink. Stir 'em once or twice, then pour in the rest of the beer and close the lid. Wait about two or three minutes, then open the pot lid again. Shrimp ought to be good and pink. If they're not, stir 'em once more and cook 'em another minute or two to make sure *all* the shrimp are pink.

Right now — take it all out with a big spoon with holes in it, and serve it up on a big plate with some lemon wedges and corn on the cob. Watch how that steam comes off the dish!

Looks good, don't it? Now put the plate on your table with a little bowl of melted lemon butter 'side each plate.

Fact is, people ought to be able to figger out what to do next. But in case they can't, tell 'em to peel the shrimp and dip 'em in the lemon butter bowl with their fingers and eat 'em (the shrimp, that is).

Tell 'em not to eat the shrimp *hulls*, neither, or to throw 'em in the lemon butter bowls.

Some folks say to serve 'em with a good white wine. But Mama Blue likes 'em with beer. Me, I like 'em with Dr Pepper.

Just about every time me and Li'l Forrest fix this dish, Ol' Bubba comes back to me, like in a dream, the two of us out on a shrimp boat just like we planned on. Water all flat and calm of an early mornin', and them seagulls whirlin' overhead, and the sun just risin' up off the Gulf of Mexico, nets draggin', motors strainin', and Ol' Bubba smilin' — just like he said he would. But dreams is just dreams, I guess.

But let me say this: When we all used to sit around the table with them steamin' shrimp… me and Bubba's mama and Lieutenant Dan and Jenny — Jenny was… well, she was somethin' else — but anyway, we'd all drink a little toast to Good Ol' Bubba. And let me say this, too: When I remember back on it all, and look up at night and see the stars, I'm always thinkin' one thing…

That me and Bubba and Jenny and Lieutenant Dan — at least we didn't lead no humdrum life.

YOURS TRULY,
FORREST GUMP

you can bake it

Millionaire Stuffed Shrimp

1	dozen unpeeled jumbo fresh shrimp
6	cups water
1	medium onion, finely chopped
½	medium-size green pepper, finely chopped
½	cup finely chopped celery
½	cup butter or margarine, melted and divided
1	pound fresh lump crabmeat, drained
1	large egg, lightly beaten
¾	cup crushed saltine crackers
½	cup mayonnaise
1	tablespoon prepared mustard
2	teaspoons Worcestershire sauce
⅛	teaspoon ground red pepper
	Paprika

Peel and devein shrimp, leaving tails intact; cut a slit almost through back of shrimp, using a paring knife. Open shrimp, and flatten. Bring water to a boil. Add shrimp; cook 1 minute. Drain; place in a shallow pan.

Cook onion, green pepper, and celery in ¼ cup butter in a skillet, stirring often, until tender. Combine crabmeat and next 6 ingredients in a bowl, stirring gently. Stir in vegetable mixture. Top each shrimp with 3 tablespoons crabmeat mixture; sprinkle with paprika. Drizzle ¼ cup butter over top. Bake, uncovered, at 350° for 20 minutes. Broil 5½ inches from heat (with electric oven door partially opened) 6 minutes, basting twice with pan drippings. Yield: 4 appetizer servings.

Alabama-Style Shrimp Bake

1	cup butter or margarine, melted
¾	cup lemon juice
¾	cup Worcestershire sauce
1	tablespoon salt
1	tablespoon coarsely ground pepper
1	teaspoon dried rosemary
⅛	teaspoon ground red pepper
1	tablespoon hot sauce
3	cloves garlic, minced
2½	pounds unpeeled large or jumbo fresh shrimp
2	lemons, thinly sliced
1	medium onion, thinly sliced

Garnish: fresh rosemary sprigs

Combine first 9 ingredients in a small bowl; set aside.

Rinse shrimp with cold water; drain well. Layer shrimp, lemon slices, and onion slices in an ungreased 13- x 9- x 2-inch baking dish. Pour butter mixture over shrimp.

Bake, uncovered, at 400° for 20 to 25 minutes or until shrimp turn pink, basting occasionally with pan juices. Garnish, if desired. Yield: 6 servings.

"Mama always said, life is like a box of chocolates. You never know what you're gonna get."

Shrimp Quickie

3	pounds unpeeled large fresh shrimp
1	(8-ounce) bottle Italian salad dressing
¼	cup butter or margarine, melted
¼	cup fresh lemon juice
¼	teaspoon freshly ground pepper

Peel and devein shrimp, leaving tails intact. Combine Italian dressing and remaining ingredients in a 13- x 9- x 2-inch baking dish. Add shrimp, stirring well. Bake, uncovered, at 325° for 25 minutes or until shrimp turn pink, stirring occasionally. Yield: 6 to 8 servings.

Shrimp Dijonnaise

¾	pound unpeeled large fresh shrimp
½	cup lemon juice
¼	cup butter or margarine, melted
2	tablespoons vegetable oil
2	tablespoons Dijon mustard
1	tablespoon Worcestershire sauce
8	cloves garlic, minced

Peel and devein shrimp, leaving tails intact. Combine lemon juice and remaining ingredients in a shallow dish; add shrimp, stirring well. Cover and chill 4 hours. Place shrimp on a greased rack of a broiler pan. Broil 5½ inches from heat (with electric oven door partially opened) 4 minutes or until shrimp turn pink. Yield: 2 servings.

"Mama said you could tell an awful lot about a person by their shoes… where they've been and where they're going. I've worn lots of shoes."

Bubba's Beer-Broiled Shrimp

2	pounds unpeeled large fresh shrimp
¾	cup beer
2	tablespoons chopped fresh parsley
2	tablespoons vegetable oil
1	tablespoon plus 1 teaspoon Worcestershire sauce
1	clove garlic, minced
⅛	teaspoon salt
¼	teaspoon pepper
⅛	teaspoon hot sauce

Peel and devein shrimp, leaving tails intact. Combine beer and remaining ingredients in a large shallow dish; add shrimp, stirring gently to coat. Cover and marinate in refrigerator 2 to 3 hours, stirring occasionally.

Drain shrimp, discarding marinade. Thread neck and tail of each shrimp onto six 14-inch skewers so shrimp will lie flat; place skewers on a lightly greased rack of a broiler pan. Broil 5½ inches from heat (with electric oven door partially opened) 3 minutes; turn and broil an additional 1 to 2 minutes or until shrimp turn pink. Yield: 6 servings.

Bayou la Batre Shrimp Mornay

1¼	pounds unpeeled large fresh shrimp
½	pound sea scallops
½	cup Chablis or other dry white wine
2	(10-ounce) containers Standard oysters, drained
½	cup dry white vermouth
1	tablespoon finely chopped onion
¼	cup plus 2 tablespoons butter or margarine, melted
¼	cup all-purpose flour
2	cups milk
⅔	cup grated Parmesan cheese
½	cup (2 ounces) shredded Gruyère cheese
½	cup (2 ounces) shredded Swiss cheese
¼	teaspoon salt
¼	teaspoon pepper
⅛	teaspoon ground nutmeg
½	cup crushed round buttery crackers
¼	cup butter or margarine, melted
	Paprika

Garnish: chopped fresh parsley

Peel and devein shrimp. Combine shrimp, scallops, and wine in a medium skillet; bring to a boil. Reduce heat, and simmer 3 minutes; drain well. Set shrimp and scallops aside. Repeat procedure with oysters and vermouth. Combine shrimp, scallops, and oysters, and spoon evenly into 4 lightly greased individual baking dishes.

Cook onion in ¼ cup plus 2 tablespoons butter in a heavy saucepan over medium-high heat, stirring constantly, until tender. Reduce heat to low; add flour, stirring until smooth. Cook 1 minute, stirring constantly. Gradually add milk; cook over medium heat, stirring constantly, until mixture is thickened and bubbly. Add cheeses, salt, pepper, and nutmeg, stirring until cheeses melt. Spoon sauce evenly over seafood mixture.

Combine cracker crumbs and ¼ cup melted butter; sprinkle evenly over casseroles. Sprinkle with paprika. Bake, uncovered, at 350° for 20 to 30 minutes or until golden and thoroughly heated. Garnish, if desired. Yield: 4 servings.

"Our house was never empty 'cause there was always someone coming and going."

Jenny's Little Shrimp Casseroles

9	cups water
3	pounds unpeeled medium-size fresh shrimp
1	tablespoon lemon juice
½	cup chopped green pepper
¼	cup chopped onion
2	tablespoons butter or margarine, melted
1	(10¾-ounce) can cream of celery soup, undiluted
1	cup half-and-half
¼	cup dry sherry
½	teaspoon salt
½	teaspoon ground white pepper
3	cups cooked rice
	Paprika

Garnish: fresh parsley sprigs

Bring water to a boil; add shrimp, and cook 3 to 5 minutes or until shrimp turn pink. Drain; rinse with cold water. Chill. Peel and devein shrimp. Reserve 6 shrimp. Combine remaining shrimp and lemon juice; set aside.

    Cook green pepper and onion in butter in a skillet over medium-high heat, stirring constantly, until tender.

    Combine soup, half-and-half, sherry, salt, and pepper in a large bowl; stir in shrimp, vegetable mixture, and rice. Spoon into lightly greased individual au gratin dishes. Sprinkle with paprika. Bake, uncovered, at 350° for 15 to 20 minutes or until hot and bubbly. Garnish with reserved shrimp and parsley, if desired. Yield: 6 servings.

"Mama always had a way of explaining things so I could understand them. Mama was a real smart lady."

Alabama-Style Shrimp Bake, page 13

Grilled Orange Shrimp Salad, page 30

Mama's Shrimp Spaghetti

4½	cups water
1½	pounds unpeeled medium-size fresh shrimp
½	(7-ounce) package vermicelli or thin spaghetti
⅓	cup butter or margarine
⅓	cup all-purpose flour
⅔	cup chicken broth
⅔	cup whipping cream
¾	cup (3 ounces) shredded Swiss cheese
2½	tablespoons dry sherry
½	teaspoon salt
⅛	teaspoon ground white pepper
2	tablespoons grated Parmesan cheese
2	tablespoons slivered almonds

Bring water to a boil; add shrimp, and cook 3 to 5 minutes or until shrimp turn pink. Drain well; rinse with cold water. Chill. Peel and devein shrimp; set aside.

Cook vermicelli according to directions; drain.

Melt butter in a saucepan over low heat; stir in flour. Cook 1 minute, stirring constantly. Gradually add broth and cream; cook over medium heat, stirring constantly, until thickened. Stir in Swiss cheese, sherry, salt, and pepper. Remove from heat; stir in shrimp and vermicelli.

Spoon mixture into a greased 2-quart casserole; sprinkle with Parmesan cheese and almonds. Bake, uncovered, at 350° for 20 minutes or until heated. Broil 5½ inches from heat (with electric oven door partially opened) 6 minutes or until browned. Yield: 6 servings.

Shrimp and Noodle Bake

6	cups water
2	pounds unpeeled large fresh shrimp
1	(8-ounce) package medium egg noodles
½	cup sliced green onions
¼	cup chopped green pepper
2	tablespoons butter or margarine, melted
2	(10¾-ounce) cans cream of mushroom soup, undiluted
1	(8-ounce) carton plain yogurt
½	cup (2 ounces) shredded Cheddar cheese
1½	teaspoons chopped fresh dill or ½ teaspoon dried dillweed
½	teaspoon ground white pepper
¼	teaspoon salt

Bring water to a boil; add shrimp, and cook 3 minutes or until shrimp begin to turn pink. Drain well; rinse with cold water. Chill. Peel and devein shrimp. Chop half of shrimp, leaving remaining shrimp whole. Set shrimp aside.

Cook noodles according to directions; drain.

Cook green onions and green pepper in butter in a Dutch oven over medium-high heat, stirring constantly, until tender. Add soup and next 5 ingredients. Gently stir in chopped shrimp and noodles. Spoon mixture into a lightly greased shallow 2½-quart casserole. Arrange whole shrimp on top of casserole.

Bake, covered, at 350° for 35 minutes or until thoroughly heated. Yield: 6 servings.

"Remember what I told you, Forrest… you're no different than anybody else is."

Shrimp Pizza Wedges

1½	cups water
½	pound unpeeled medium-size fresh shrimp
2	teaspoons lemon juice
1	(8-ounce) package cream cheese, softened
1	cup (4 ounces) shredded Cheddar or Monterey Jack cheese
4	green onions, chopped
2	jalapeño peppers, seeded and chopped
2	cloves garlic, minced
2	tablespoons chopped fresh cilantro
1	teaspoon ground cumin
1	teaspoon chili powder
9	(6-inch) whole wheat flour tortillas

Garnishes: whole shrimp, fresh cilantro sprigs

Bring water to a boil; add shrimp, and cook 3 to 5 minutes or until shrimp turn pink. Drain well; rinse with cold water. Chill. Peel and devein shrimp. Combine shrimp and lemon juice; cover and chill 30 minutes.

Position knife blade in food processor bowl; add chilled shrimp mixture, cream cheese, and next 7 ingredients. Process 1 minute or until smooth, scraping down sides occasionally.

Place tortillas on baking sheets; spread about ¼ cup shrimp mixture on each tortilla. Bake at 350° for 8 to 10 minutes or until edges begin to brown. Cut each into 8 wedges. Garnish, if desired. Serve warm. Yield: 6 dozen.

Shrimp-Gruyère Cheesecake

1¼	cups crushed round buttery crackers
¼	cup butter or margarine, melted
1½	pounds unpeeled medium-size fresh shrimp
⅓	cup minced green pepper
⅓	cup minced sweet red pepper
¼	cup minced onion
1	large clove garlic, minced
3	tablespoons butter or margarine, melted
2	(8-ounce) packages cream cheese, softened
½	cup mayonnaise
4	large eggs
⅓	cup milk
1¼	cups (5 ounces) shredded Gruyère or Swiss cheese
1	teaspoon ground white pepper
	Italian Tomato Sauce

Garnishes: sweet red pepper strips, whole shrimp, fresh basil sprigs

Combine cracker crumbs and ¼ cup melted butter; press mixture evenly onto bottom of a 9-inch springform pan. Set aside.

Peel, devein, and chop shrimp. Cook shrimp and next 4 ingredients in 3 tablespoons butter in a large skillet over medium-high heat, stirring constantly, 4 to 5 minutes or until shrimp are done and vegetables are tender. Drain well, and set aside.

"Mama always told me miracles happen every day. Now some people don't think so. But they do."

Beat cream cheese and mayonnaise at high speed of an electric mixer until creamy; add eggs, one at a time, beating after each addition. Gradually add milk, beating well at low speed just until blended. Stir in shrimp mixture, Gruyère cheese, and white pepper.

Pour mixture into prepared pan. Bake at 300° for 1 hour and 20 minutes or until set. Turn oven off, and partially open oven door; leave cheesecake in oven 1 hour.

Cool completely on a wire rack; cover and chill at least 8 hours. Serve with warm Italian Tomato Sauce. Garnish, if desired. Yield: 8 servings.

Italian Tomato Sauce
- ¼ cup chopped onion
- 1 clove garlic, minced
- 1 tablespoon olive oil
- 2 (14-ounce) cans tomatoes, drained and chopped
- 1½ teaspoons dried Italian seasoning
- 1 bay leaf

Cook onion and garlic in oil in a large skillet over medium-high heat, stirring constantly, until tender. Add tomatoes and remaining ingredients; bring to a boil. Reduce heat, and simmer, uncovered, 20 minutes or until most of liquid evaporates, stirring occasionally. Remove and discard bay leaf. Yield: about 2 cups.

Miniature Shrimp Quiches

1	cup (4 ounces) shredded Swiss cheese
½	cup finely chopped cooked shrimp
2	tablespoons chopped fresh chives
½	teaspoon dried thyme
	Pastry Shells
2	large eggs, beaten
½	cup half-and-half
¼	teaspoon salt
¼	teaspoon pepper
¼	teaspoon ground nutmeg
	Dash of hot sauce

Combine first 4 ingredients; spoon evenly into Pastry Shells. Combine eggs and remaining ingredients, stirring well; pour mixture evenly into Pastry Shells. Bake at 350° for 30 to 35 minutes or until set. Yield: 3 dozen.

Pastry Shells

½	cup butter or margarine, softened
½	(8-ounce) package cream cheese, softened
1½	cups all-purpose flour
¼	teaspoon salt

Beat butter and cream cheese at medium speed of an electric mixer until well blended; stir in flour and salt. Cover and chill 1 hour. Shape chilled dough into 1-inch balls. Place in ungreased miniature (1¾-inch) muffin pans, shaping each ball into a shell. Yield: 3 dozen.

"... I remember the first time I heard the sweetest voice in the whole wide world. She was an angel. I had never seen anything so beautiful in all my life."

you can
barbecue it

Lemon-Garlic Shrimp Kabobs

2	pounds unpeeled jumbo fresh shrimp
1	medium onion, diced
4	cloves garlic, minced
½	cup vegetable oil
¼	cup plus 2 tablespoons lemon juice
3	tablespoons soy sauce
2	teaspoons ground ginger

Peel shrimp, leaving tails intact; devein, if desired. Combine onion and remaining ingredients in a large shallow dish; add shrimp, stirring gently to coat. Cover and marinate in refrigerator 2 to 3 hours, stirring occasionally.

Drain shrimp, discarding marinade. Thread neck and tail of each shrimp onto six 14-inch skewers so shrimp will lie flat. Grill shrimp, uncovered, over medium-hot coals (350° to 400°) 3 to 4 minutes on each side or until shrimp turn pink. Yield: 4 to 6 servings.

Lime-Barbecued Shrimp

2	pounds unpeeled jumbo fresh shrimp
¾	cup butter or margarine, melted
¼	cup fresh lime juice

Peel shrimp, leaving tails intact; devein, if desired. Combine butter and lime juice in a small saucepan. Dip shrimp in butter mixture. Thread neck and tail of each shrimp onto six 14-inch skewers so shrimp will lie flat.

Grill shrimp, covered, over medium-hot coals (350° to 400°) 3 to 4 minutes on each side or until shrimp turn pink. Bring any remaining butter mixture to a boil over high heat; remove from heat, and serve with shrimp. Yield: 4 to 6 servings.

Medal of Honor Shrimp Grill

2	pounds unpeeled large fresh shrimp
⅓	cup dry sherry
⅓	cup sesame oil
⅓	cup soy sauce
½	teaspoon sugar
¼	teaspoon garlic powder
¼	teaspoon ground ginger

Peel shrimp, leaving tails intact; devein, if desired. Combine sherry and remaining ingredients in a large shallow dish; add shrimp, stirring gently. Cover and marinate in refrigerator 2 to 3 hours, stirring occasionally.

Drain shrimp, reserving marinade. Bring marinade to a boil over high heat; remove from heat, and set aside. Thread neck and tail of each shrimp onto six 14-inch skewers so shrimp will lie flat. Grill shrimp, uncovered, over medium-hot coals (350° to 400°) 3 to 4 minutes on each side or until shrimp turn pink, basting frequently with reserved marinade. Yield: 4 to 6 servings.

"I'm Forrest, Forrest Gump... people call me Forrest Gump."

Grilled Orange Shrimp Salad

30	unpeeled large fresh shrimp
1	cup orange juice
3	tablespoons chopped fresh basil
1	head Bibb lettuce
4	cups mixed baby lettuces
	Cilantro-Lime Vinaigrette
15	yellow pear tomatoes, halved
15	red pear tomatoes, halved
2	cucumbers, thinly sliced

Peel and devein shrimp. Combine orange juice and basil; add shrimp. Cover and chill 1 hour, stirring occasionally.

Drain shrimp; discard marinade. Thread neck and tail of each shrimp onto six 14-inch skewers so shrimp will lie flat. Grill, covered, over medium-hot coals (350° to 400°) 3 to 4 minutes on each side or until done. Combine lettuces; toss with vinaigrette. Arrange on salad plates; top with shrimp, tomato, and cucumber. Yield: 6 servings.

Cilantro-Lime Vinaigrette

¼	cup sugar
¼	cup extra-virgin olive oil
2	tablespoons lime juice
1½	teaspoons chopped fresh cilantro
1	shallot, minced
1	clove garlic, minced

Combine ingredients. Cover tightly; shake. Yield: ¾ cup.

"People call me Bubba… just like one of them good ol' rednecked boys. If you can believe that."

Jenny's Southwestern Shrimp

2	pounds unpeeled large fresh shrimp
⅓	cup lime juice
⅓	cup olive oil
2	tablespoons chopped fresh cilantro
2	tablespoons tequila
¼	teaspoon salt
¼	teaspoon pepper
1	jalapeño pepper, seeded and chopped
1	clove garlic, minced

Peel shrimp, leaving tails intact; devein, if desired. Combine lime juice and remaining ingredients in a shallow dish; add shrimp, stirring gently to coat. Cover and marinate in refrigerator 2 to 3 hours, stirring occasionally.

Drain shrimp, reserving marinade. Bring marinade to a boil over high heat; remove from heat, and set aside. Thread neck and tail of each shrimp onto six 14-inch skewers so shrimp will lie flat. Grill shrimp, uncovered, over medium-hot coals (350° to 400°) 3 to 4 minutes on each side or until shrimp turn pink, basting frequently with reserved marinade. Yield: 4 to 6 servings.

Shrimp and Vegetable Kabobs

1½	pounds unpeeled medium-size fresh shrimp
1	(8-ounce) bottle Italian salad dressing
¼	cup grated Parmesan cheese
¼	cup water
½	teaspoon dried crushed red pepper
8	boiling onions
16	small fresh mushrooms
2	small zucchini, cut into 1-inch slices
1	large sweet red pepper, cut into 1-inch pieces

Peel shrimp, leaving tails intact; devein, if desired. Combine salad dressing and next 3 ingredients in a large shallow dish; add shrimp, stirring gently to coat. Cover shrimp, and marinate in refrigerator 3 to 4 hours, stirring occasionally.

Parboil onions 5 minutes; drain well, and set aside. Drain shrimp, reserving marinade. Bring marinade to a boil over high heat; remove from heat, and set aside.

Alternate shrimp and vegetables on eight 12-inch skewers. Grill, uncovered, over medium-hot coals (350° to 400°) 3 to 4 minutes on each side or until shrimp turn pink, turning and basting frequently with reserved marinade. Yield: 4 servings.

"I'm gonna lean up against you and you just lean against me and that way we won't have to sleep with our heads in the mud."

you can boil it

Spicy Shrimp Dip

1½	cups water
½	pound unpeeled medium-size fresh shrimp
1	(3-ounce) package cream cheese, softened
1	(8-ounce) carton sour cream
1	(0.7-ounce) envelope Italian salad dressing mix
2	tablespoons finely chopped green pepper
2	teaspoons lemon juice

Bring water to a boil; add shrimp, and cook 3 to 5 minutes or until shrimp turn pink. Drain well; rinse with cold water. Chill. Peel, devein, and chop shrimp.

Beat cream cheese at medium speed of an electric mixer until creamy. Stir in sour cream, shrimp, and remaining ingredients. Cover and chill at least 1 hour. Serve with fresh vegetables. Yield: 1⅔ cups.

"You know what I'm thinkin' about, Forrest? Shrimp...! Shrimp...! What it's like to be out on the water. Nothing to worry about but the wind and the sea... makes you feel alive, Forrest, like no other feelin' in the world."

Real Smooth Shrimp Butter

2½	cups water
¾	pound unpeeled medium-size fresh shrimp
½	cup butter, softened
1	large hard-cooked egg, coarsely chopped
1	(3-ounce) package cream cheese, softened
¼	cup coarsely chopped onion
¼	cup mayonnaise or salad dressing
⅛	teaspoon salt
⅛	teaspoon pepper
⅛	teaspoon Worcestershire sauce
1	clove garlic

Bring water to a boil; add shrimp, and cook 3 to 5 minutes or until shrimp turn pink. Drain well; rinse with cold water. Chill. Peel, devein, and coarsely chop shrimp.

Position knife blade in food processor bowl; add shrimp, butter, and remaining ingredients. Process until smooth, scraping down sides occasionally.

Line a 2-cup mold or bowl with heavy-duty plastic wrap, allowing plastic wrap to extend over edges at least 2 inches. Spoon shrimp mixture into mold; cover and chill at least 4 hours.

Invert mold onto serving plate. Remove mold, and carefully peel away plastic wrap. Smooth surface with a knife, if necessary. Let stand at room temperature 20 to 30 minutes before serving. Serve with assorted crackers. Yield: 1⅔ cups.

Zippy Shrimp Spread

3	cups water
1	pound unpeeled medium-size fresh shrimp
2	(3-ounce) packages cream cheese, softened
1/3	cup catsup
1	teaspoon grated onion
1	teaspoon prepared horseradish
1/2	teaspoon ground red pepper
1/2	teaspoon Worcestershire sauce

Bring water to a boil; add shrimp, and cook 3 to 5 minutes or until shrimp turn pink. Drain well; rinse with cold water. Chill. Peel and devein shrimp. Reserve 3 shrimp for garnish; coarsely chop remaining shrimp. Set aside.

Combine cream cheese and remaining ingredients in a mixing bowl; beat at medium speed of an electric mixer until blended. Stir in chopped shrimp. Spoon shrimp mixture into a small serving bowl; cover and chill at least 2 hours. Garnish with reserved whole shrimp. Serve with assorted crackers. Yield: 1¼ cups.

Shrimp and Vegetable Kabobs, page 32

Shrimp 'n' Chicken Gumbo, page 58

Mighty Nice Shrimp Cheese Ball

3	cups water
1	pound unpeeled medium-size fresh shrimp
1	(8-ounce) package cream cheese, softened
1	tablespoon prepared horseradish
1	tablespoon lemon juice
2	teaspoons grated onion
1	teaspoon liquid smoke
¼	cup chopped pecans, toasted
2	tablespoons chopped fresh parsley

Bring water to a boil; add shrimp, and cook 3 to 5 minutes or until shrimp turn pink. Drain well; rinse with cold water. Chill. Peel, devein, and chop shrimp.

Combine shrimp, cream cheese, and next 4 ingredients in a bowl; stir well. Cover and chill 1 hour. Shape shrimp mixture into a ball; cover and chill thoroughly.

Combine chopped pecans and parsley; roll cheese ball in pecan mixture. Serve with assorted crackers. Yield: 1 (4-inch) cheese ball.

"Bubba was my best friend… and you don't find that very often."

Layered Shrimp Appetizer

2½	cups water
¾	pound unpeeled medium-size fresh shrimp
1	(8-ounce) package cream cheese, softened
½	cup sour cream
¼	teaspoon onion salt
	Dash of ground red pepper
¼	cup plus 2 tablespoons chili sauce
1½	teaspoons Worcestershire sauce
¾	teaspoon lemon juice
½	teaspoon prepared horseradish

Garnishes: fresh parsley sprigs, lemon slices

Bring water to a boil; add shrimp, and cook 3 to 5 minutes or until shrimp turn pink. Drain well; rinse with cold water. Chill. Peel and devein shrimp. Chop two-thirds of shrimp, leaving remaining shrimp whole. Cover and chill chopped and whole shrimp.
 Beat cream cheese at medium speed of an electric mixer until creamy. Add sour cream, onion salt, and red pepper, beating until smooth. Spread mixture onto serving platter, shaping into a 5-inch circle. Cover and chill at least 30 minutes.
 Combine chili sauce, Worcestershire sauce, lemon juice, and horseradish; stir well, and spread over cream cheese round. Sprinkle chopped shrimp over chili sauce mixture; top with whole shrimp. Garnish, if desired. Cover and chill. Serve with assorted crackers. Yield: 3 cups.

Bubba Gump's Shrimp Cocktail

6	cups water
2	tablespoons salt
2	bay leaves
1	lemon, halved
1	stalk celery, cut into 3-inch pieces
2	pounds unpeeled medium-size fresh shrimp
4	cups shredded lettuce (optional)
	Bubba's Cocktail Sauce (page 103)

Garnish: lemon wedges

Combine first 5 ingredients in a Dutch oven. Bring to a boil; add shrimp, and cook 3 to 5 minutes or until shrimp turn pink. Drain well; rinse with cold water. Chill. Peel and devein shrimp.

    Arrange lettuce on individual serving plates, if desired. Top with shrimp. Serve with Bubba's Cocktail Sauce. Garnish, if desired. Yield: 8 to 10 appetizer servings.

"Forrest, how'd you like to go into the shrimpin' business with me?"

Shrimp with Jalapeño Cheese

2	pounds unpeeled large fresh shrimp
6	cups water
1	(8-ounce) package cream cheese, softened
2	pickled jalapeño peppers, seeded and finely chopped
1	clove garlic, minced
2	teaspoons chopped fresh cilantro
¼	teaspoon salt
⅛	teaspoon pepper

Peel shrimp, leaving tail and first joint of shell intact; cut a deep slit down the length of the outside curve of each shrimp, and devein.

Bring water to a boil; add shrimp, and cook 3 to 5 minutes or until shrimp turn pink. Drain well; rinse with cold water. Chill.

Combine cream cheese and remaining ingredients; beat well. Fill a decorating bag fitted with metal tip No. 21 with cream cheese mixture. Pipe filling lengthwise into the slits in the shrimp. Yield: 16 to 18 appetizer servings.

"I've got it all figured out. So many pounds of shrimps to pay off the boat, so much for the gas. We can live on the boat. I'll be the captain, and we'll work it together."

Lt. Dan's Lemon Shrimp

20	unpeeled large fresh shrimp
¼	cup butter or margarine
¾	cup fresh crabmeat, drained and flaked
¼	cup dry white vermouth
2	tablespoons minced fresh parsley
1½	tablespoons lemon juice
2	cloves garlic, minced

Garnishes: fresh parsley sprigs, lemon wedges

Peel and devein shrimp, leaving tails intact; set aside.
    Melt butter in a large skillet over medium heat; add shrimp, crabmeat, and next 4 ingredients. Bring to a boil; reduce heat, and simmer, uncovered, 4 to 5 minutes. Spoon mixture evenly into 4 individual serving dishes, arranging shrimp around crabmeat. Garnish, if desired. Yield: 4 appetizer servings.

Smiley Face Shrimp

3	quarts water
1	large lemon, sliced
4	pounds unpeeled large fresh shrimp
2	cups vegetable oil
¼	cup hot sauce
1	tablespoon minced garlic
1	tablespoon olive oil
1½	teaspoons salt
1½	teaspoons Old Bay seasoning
1½	teaspoons dried basil
1½	teaspoons dried oregano
1½	teaspoons dried thyme
1½	teaspoons minced fresh parsley

Bring water and lemon to a boil; add shrimp, and cook 3 to 5 minutes or until shrimp turn pink. Drain well; rinse with cold water. Chill. Peel and devein shrimp. Place shrimp in a large shallow dish.

Combine vegetable oil and remaining ingredients; stir well, and pour over shrimp. Cover and chill 8 hours. Drain before serving. Yield: 25 appetizer servings.

Camouflage Shrimp-in-a-Pickle

7½	cups water
2½	pounds unpeeled medium-size fresh shrimp
3	medium onions, sliced
1	cup vegetable oil
½	cup red wine vinegar
½	cup tarragon vinegar
2	tablespoons sugar
2½	tablespoons capers with juice
1	tablespoon lemon juice
1	tablespoon Worcestershire sauce
½	teaspoon salt
¾	teaspoon hot sauce
8	bay leaves, broken

Bring water to a boil; add shrimp, and cook 3 to 5 minutes or until shrimp turn pink. Drain well; rinse with cold water. Chill. Peel and devein shrimp.

Layer shrimp and onion in an airtight container. Combine oil and remaining ingredients. Pour over shrimp and onion. Cover and chill 24 hours, stirring occasionally. Drain before serving. Yield: 10 appetizer servings.

"Split everything right down the middle… and all the shrimps you can eat."

Feather Soufflé Roll

¼	cup plus 2 tablespoons all-purpose flour
1½	cups milk
3	egg yolks
¾	teaspoon salt
⅛	teaspoon ground white pepper
⅛	teaspoon ground nutmeg
4	egg whites
	Shrimp Filling

Garnishes: whole shrimp, fresh parsley sprigs

Grease bottom and sides of a 15- x 10- x 1-inch jellyroll pan with vegetable oil. Line bottom of pan with wax paper, allowing paper to extend beyond ends of pan. Grease wax paper; flour wax paper and sides of pan. Set aside.

 Combine flour and ½ cup milk in a small saucepan, stirring until well blended. Stir in remaining 1 cup milk; cook over medium heat, stirring constantly, until thickened. Beat egg yolks in a small mixing bowl at high speed of an electric mixer until thick and pale. Gradually stir about one-fourth of hot mixture into yolks; add to remaining hot mixture, stirring constantly. Stir in salt, pepper, and nutmeg. Transfer mixture to large bowl, and let cool.

 Beat egg whites until stiff but not dry; fold into milk mixture. Spread evenly in prepared pan; bake at 375° for 20 to 25 minutes or until lightly browned.

 Remove from oven; loosen edges of soufflé with a metal spatula. Immediately cover pan with a dampened

"Bubba was my best good friend. And even I know that's something you can't just find around the corner."

cotton towel, and invert pan and towel together, turning soufflé out onto towel. Carefully peel off wax paper.

Cover soufflé with a clean piece of wax paper, and starting at long side, roll up soufflé, wax paper, and towel together. Cool completely on a wire rack; chill 3 to 4 hours.

Carefully unroll soufflé; spread with Shrimp Filling. Roll up tightly; wrap in plastic wrap. Chill 3 hours. Remove plastic wrap, and cut into 27 (½-inch) slices, using an electric knife. Garnish, if desired. Yield: 9 appetizer servings.

Shrimp Filling
1½ cups water
½ pound unpeeled medium-size fresh shrimp
2 (3-ounce) packages cream cheese, softened
2 tablespoons sour cream
1 teaspoon prepared horseradish
3 drops of hot sauce
Dash of salt
Dash of garlic powder
2 tablespoons chopped green onions

Bring water to a boil; add shrimp, and cook 3 to 5 minutes or until shrimp turn pink. Drain well; rinse with cold water. Cover and chill. Peel, devein, and chop shrimp; set aside.

Combine cream cheese and next 5 ingredients in a medium mixing bowl; beat at medium speed of an electric mixer until smooth. Stir in chopped shrimp and green onions. Yield: about 1½ cups.

Uptown Shrimp Salad

3	cups water
1	pound unpeeled medium-size fresh shrimp
3	tablespoons sherry wine vinegar or red wine vinegar
1	teaspoon sugar
1	teaspoon grated orange rind
1	clove garlic, crushed
⅓	cup olive oil
2	navel oranges
1	cup sliced pimiento-stuffed olives
5	cups torn Bibb lettuce
5	cups torn leaf lettuce
2	green onions, sliced

Bring water to a boil; add shrimp, and cook 3 to 5 minutes or until shrimp turn pink. Drain well; rinse with cold water. Chill. Peel and devein shrimp; set aside.

Combine vinegar and next 3 ingredients in a large bowl; gradually add olive oil, beating well with a wire whisk. Set aside.

Peel oranges, and cut into ½-inch round slices; cut slices into quarters. Add orange, shrimp, and olives to dressing; stir gently. Cover and chill at least 1 hour.

To serve, add lettuces and green onions to shrimp mixture; toss gently. Yield: 8 servings.

Mama's Best Shrimp Louis

6	cups water
2	pounds unpeeled medium-size fresh shrimp
½	cup mayonnaise or salad dressing
2	tablespoons chopped green onions
2	tablespoons chopped green pepper
1	large hard-cooked egg, finely chopped
1	tablespoon chopped pimiento
½	teaspoon lemon juice
½	teaspoon salt
⅛	teaspoon pepper
	Curly leaf lettuce
	Shredded iceberg lettuce

Bring water to a boil; add shrimp, and cook 3 to 5 minutes or until shrimp turn pink. Drain well; rinse with cold water. Chill. Peel and devein shrimp. Cover and chill thoroughly.

Combine mayonnaise and next 7 ingredients; stir well. Pour mayonnaise mixture over shrimp, and toss gently. Line a shell-shaped bowl or salad bowl with leaf lettuce; top with shredded iceberg lettuce. Spoon shrimp mixture evenly over shredded lettuce. Yield: 6 servings.

"If I'd known this was going to be the last thing I was going to say to Bubba, I would have thought of something better to say."

Mrs. Blue's Shrimp Salad

4½	cups water
1½	pounds unpeeled large fresh shrimp
½	cup chopped green pepper
½	cup sliced pimiento-stuffed olives
½	cup commercial Italian salad dressing
¼	cup chopped celery
3	tablespoons sweet pickle relish
2	tablespoons olive oil
2	teaspoons minced fresh parsley
1½	teaspoons lemon juice
1	green onion, minced
	Curly leaf lettuce
	Shredded iceberg lettuce

Bring water to a boil; add shrimp, and cook 3 to 5 minutes or until shrimp turn pink. Drain well; rinse with cold water. Chill. Peel and devein shrimp. Place shrimp in a large shallow dish. Combine green pepper and next 8 ingredients; pour over shrimp, stirring gently. Cover and marinate in refrigerator 2 to 3 hours, stirring occasionally.

Arrange leaf lettuce on individual serving plates; top with shredded iceberg lettuce. Spoon shrimp mixture evenly over shredded lettuce. Yield: 4 servings.

"Now the only good thing about being wounded is the ice cream. They gave me all the ice cream I could eat..."

Oriental Shrimp Salad

4½	cups water
1½	pounds unpeeled medium-size fresh shrimp
1	cup fresh bean sprouts
1	(8-ounce) can sliced water chestnuts, drained
¼	cup chopped green onions
¼	cup chopped celery
¾	cup mayonnaise or salad dressing
1	tablespoon lemon juice
1	tablespoon soy sauce
¼	teaspoon ground ginger
1	cup chow mein noodles, divided
	Lettuce leaves

Bring water to a boil; add shrimp, and cook 3 to 5 minutes or until shrimp turn pink. Drain well; rinse with cold water. Chill. Peel, devein, and chop shrimp.

Combine shrimp, bean sprouts, water chestnuts, green onions, and celery in a bowl. Combine mayonnaise and next 3 ingredients; stir well. Add mayonnaise mixture to shrimp mixture, tossing gently. Cover and chill.

Just before serving, stir in ¾ cup noodles. Spoon onto individual lettuce-lined plates, and sprinkle with remaining ¼ cup noodles. Yield: 4 servings.

Caribbean Shrimp-Bean Salad

1	(15-ounce) can black beans, rinsed and drained
1	small green pepper, finely chopped
½	cup sliced celery
½	cup sliced purple onion, separated into rings
2	tablespoons chopped fresh cilantro
⅔	cup picante sauce
¼	cup lime juice
¼	teaspoon salt
2	tablespoons vegetable oil
2	tablespoons honey
6	cups water
2	pounds unpeeled medium-size fresh shrimp
	Lettuce leaves

Garnish: cherry tomato halves

Combine first 10 ingredients; toss gently. Cover and chill 8 hours, stirring occasionally.
 Bring water to a boil; add shrimp, and cook 3 to 5 minutes or until shrimp turn pink. Drain well; rinse with cold water. Chill. Peel and devein shrimp.
 Arrange shrimp around edge of a lettuce-lined serving plate; spoon black bean mixture in center. Garnish, if desired. Yield: 4 servings.

Shrimp with Peas and Carrots

4½	cups water
1½	pounds unpeeled medium-size fresh shrimp
1	(12-ounce) package vermicelli, uncooked
1½	cups chopped green onions
1½	cups frozen English peas and carrots, thawed
1	cup chopped dill pickle
¼	cup minced fresh parsley
3	large hard-cooked eggs, chopped
1	(2-ounce) jar diced pimiento, drained
1	small green pepper, chopped
1	(8-ounce) carton sour cream
1	cup mayonnaise or salad dressing
¼	cup lemon juice
2	tablespoons prepared mustard
1	teaspoon celery seeds
1	teaspoon salt
¼	teaspoon pepper
	Leaf lettuce

Bring water to a boil; add shrimp, and cook 3 to 5 minutes or until shrimp turn pink. Drain well; rinse with cold water. Chill. Peel and devein shrimp.

Break vermicelli into 3-inch pieces. Cook according to directions; drain. Place in a large bowl. Stir in shrimp, green onions, and next 6 ingredients; set aside.

Combine sour cream and next 6 ingredients. Pour over shrimp mixture; toss gently. Cover and chill. Transfer to a lettuce-lined platter. Yield: 8 servings.

"When I got home I was a national celebrity... famouser even than Captain Kangaroo."

Route 19 Shrimp Chowder

1	pound unpeeled medium-size fresh shrimp
3	tablespoons butter or margarine
3	tablespoons all-purpose flour
1	tablespoon curry powder
2	cups chicken broth
2	(8-ounce) bottles clam juice
2	cups half-and-half
4	medium baking potatoes, peeled and coarsely chopped (about 4 cups)
1	pound grouper or amberjack fillets, cut into bite-size pieces

Peel and devein shrimp; set aside.

Melt butter in a large Dutch oven over low heat; add flour and curry powder, stirring until smooth. Cook 1 minute, stirring constantly. Gradually add chicken broth, stirring until smooth. Add clam juice, half-and-half, and potato; stir well. Bring to a boil; reduce heat, and simmer, uncovered, 20 minutes or until potato is tender.

Add shrimp and fish to soup mixture; cook 5 to 6 minutes or until shrimp turn pink. Serve immediately. Yield: 3½ quarts.

"I made a promise to Bubba. And when I save up enough money, I'm going into the shrimpin' business, sir. A promise is a promise, Lt. Dan."

Shrimp and Cheese Omelet, page 64

Gulf Coast Fried Shrimp, page 77

Peace March Shrimp Gazpacho

4½	cups water
1½	pounds unpeeled small fresh shrimp
2	quarts tomato juice
4	tomatoes, peeled, seeded, and chopped
2	cucumbers, peeled, seeded, and chopped
1	bunch green onions, chopped
1	avocado, peeled and chopped
1	(8-ounce) package cream cheese, cut into ½-inch cubes
¼	cup lemon juice or white wine vinegar
2	tablespoons sugar
½	teaspoon hot sauce

Garnishes: cucumber slices, sour cream, whole shrimp

Bring water to a boil; add shrimp, and cook 3 to 5 minutes or until shrimp turn pink. Drain well; rinse with cold water. Chill. Peel and devein shrimp. Reserve 10 shrimp for garnish, if desired.

 Combine remaining shrimp, tomato juice, and next 8 ingredients in a large bowl; cover and chill at least 3 hours. Garnish, if desired. Yield: 3¼ quarts.

Shrimp 'n' Chicken Gumbo

2	pounds chicken breast halves, skinned
2	quarts water
½	cup all-purpose flour
2	cups chopped onion
1¾	cups chopped celery
1½	cups chopped green pepper
½	cup chopped green onions
4	cloves garlic, minced
2	tablespoons vegetable oil
1½	teaspoons dried thyme
1	teaspoon dried oregano
½	teaspoon pepper
3	bay leaves
1	(14½-ounce) can ready-to-serve chicken broth
1	(8-ounce) can tomato paste
½	pound smoked sausage, sliced
1	pound unpeeled medium-size fresh shrimp
	Hot cooked rice

Combine chicken and water in a Dutch oven; bring to a boil. Reduce heat, and simmer, uncovered, 45 minutes or until chicken is done. Remove chicken from broth; set aside to cool. Strain broth, if desired, and transfer to a large container; set aside. Bone and chop chicken; set aside.

    Place flour in a 15- x 10- x 1-inch jellyroll pan. Bake at 350° for 45 minutes to 1 hour or until very brown, stirring every 15 minutes. Set aside.

Cook onion and next 4 ingredients in oil in Dutch oven over medium-high heat, stirring constantly, until tender. Add browned flour, thyme, and next 3 ingredients, stirring until smooth. Add reserved broth, chicken, canned broth, tomato paste, and sausage. Bring to a boil; reduce heat, and simmer, uncovered, 1 hour.

Peel and devein shrimp; add to broth mixture. Cover and simmer 10 minutes or until shrimp turn pink. Remove and discard bay leaves. Serve over rice. Yield: 4½ quarts.

"Don't you just love New Year's? It's like startin' all over. Everybody gets a second chance."

Greenbow County Okra Gumbo

1	pound fresh okra, sliced
¼	cup plus 2 tablespoons butter or margarine, melted and divided
¼	cup all-purpose flour
1	bunch green onions, sliced
½	cup chopped celery
2	cloves garlic, minced
2	quarts water
1	(16-ounce) can whole tomatoes, undrained and chopped
1	tablespoon chopped fresh parsley
1½	teaspoons salt
½	teaspoon ground red pepper
1	sprig fresh thyme
1	bay leaf
1	pound unpeeled medium-size fresh shrimp
½	pound fresh crabmeat, drained and flaked
	Hot cooked rice
	Gumbo filé (optional)

Cook okra in 2 tablespoons butter in a large skillet over medium-high heat, stirring constantly, until lightly browned. Set aside.

Combine remaining ¼ cup butter and flour in a large Dutch oven; cook over medium heat, stirring constantly, until roux is chocolate colored (20 to 25 minutes). Stir in green onions, celery, and garlic; cook, stirring constantly, until vegetables are tender. Add okra, water, and next 6

"Now, Bubba taught me everything he knew about shrimpin', but you know what I found out? Shrimpin' is tough."

ingredients. Bring to a boil; reduce heat, and simmer, uncovered, 2 hours, stirring occasionally.

Peel and devein shrimp; add shrimp and crabmeat to okra mixture. Simmer an additional 10 minutes, stirring occasionally. Remove and discard bay leaf. Serve gumbo over rice. Add gumbo filé, if desired. Yield: 2½ quarts.

Tex's Shrimp Enchilada Soup

1	pound unpeeled medium-size fresh shrimp
5	cups chicken broth
4	ounces tortilla chips
2	(4½-ounce) cans chopped green chiles, undrained
1	(10-ounce) can diced tomatoes and green chiles, undrained
2	tablespoons butter or margarine
1	medium onion, chopped
2	cloves garlic, minced
1	(8-ounce) carton sour cream
¼	cup chopped fresh cilantro
	Shredded mozzarella cheese
	Shredded Cheddar cheese

Peel and devein shrimp; set aside. Bring broth to a boil in a Dutch oven; add tortilla chips. Remove from heat; let stand 10 minutes. Position knife blade in food processor bowl; add half of broth mixture. Process until smooth, scraping down sides once. Transfer mixture to another container. Repeat procedure with remaining broth mixture. Return blended mixture to Dutch oven; stir in green chiles and diced tomatoes. Set aside.

Melt butter in a large skillet over medium-high heat. Add shrimp, onion, and garlic; cook, stirring constantly, 3 to 4 minutes or until shrimp turn pink. Stir into broth mixture; cook until heated, stirring occasionally (do not boil). Stir in sour cream and cilantro. Sprinkle each serving with cheeses. Serve immediately. Yield: 2 quarts.

Old Reliable Shrimp Stock

2	pounds unpeeled medium-size fresh shrimp with heads
3	quarts water
1	large carrot
2	stalks celery, quartered
1	medium onion, quartered
½	cup fresh thyme sprigs with stems
½	cup fresh parsley sprigs
½	cup fresh basil leaves
½	cup fresh oregano sprigs with stems
1	tablespoon dried savory

Remove heads and peel shrimp; place heads and shells in a large Dutch oven. Reserve shrimp for another use. Add water and remaining ingredients; bring to a boil. Reduce heat, and simmer, uncovered, 45 minutes. Pour mixture through a wire-mesh strainer into a container, discarding solids. Use desired amount of stock for soups and sauces, and freeze remainder for another use. Yield: 2 quarts.

"And I have to tell you… Lt. Dan took to shrimpin' like one of them ducks in water."

Shrimp and Cheese Omelet

2	large eggs
1	tablespoon water
1	tablespoon butter or margarine
¼	cup coarsely chopped cooked shrimp
3	tablespoons shredded Monterey Jack cheese
1	tablespoon sliced green onions
2	teaspoons chopped fresh parsley

Garnishes: whole shrimp, green onions

Combine eggs and water, beating with a wire whisk; set mixture aside.

Heat an 8-inch omelet pan or nonstick skillet over medium heat until hot enough to sizzle a drop of water. Add butter, and rotate pan to coat bottom. Pour egg mixture into pan. As mixture starts to cook, gently lift edges of omelet with a spatula, and tilt pan so that uncooked portion flows underneath.

Sprinkle half of omelet with shrimp and next 3 ingredients, and fold in half. Transfer omelet to a serving plate. Garnish, if desired. Serve immediately. Yield: 1 serving.

"The really good thing about meeting the President of the United States is the food. And there was just about anything you could want to eat or drink."

Gulf Shrimp and Vegetables

9	cups water
3	pounds unpeeled large fresh shrimp
1	cup sliced ripe olives
1	cup chopped green pepper
½	cup chopped celery
⅓	cup chopped sweet pickle
1	tablespoon minced fresh parsley
2	shallots, minced
2	cups commercial Italian salad dressing
¼	cup olive oil
1	tablespoon lemon juice
	Leaf lettuce

Garnish: tomato wedges

Bring water to a boil; add shrimp, and cook 3 to 5 minutes or until shrimp turn pink. Drain well; rinse with cold water. Chill. Peel and devein shrimp. Place shrimp in a large shallow dish.

Combine olives and next 8 ingredients; pour over shrimp, tossing gently to combine. Cover and chill 8 hours.

Line a serving platter with lettuce; spoon shrimp mixture over lettuce, using a slotted spoon. Garnish, if desired. Yield: 8 to 10 servings.

Four-Square Gospel Creole

1½	pounds unpeeled medium-size fresh shrimp
1	small onion, chopped
1	small green pepper, chopped
½	cup chopped celery
2	cloves garlic, minced
2	tablespoons butter or margarine, melted
1	(16-ounce) can whole tomatoes, undrained and chopped
1	(8-ounce) can tomato sauce
2	teaspoons Worcestershire sauce
½	teaspoon dried oregano
½	teaspoon dried thyme
⅛	teaspoon ground red pepper
	Hot cooked rice

Peel and devein shrimp; set aside. Cook onion, green pepper, celery, and garlic in butter in a Dutch oven over medium heat, stirring constantly, until tender. Stir in tomatoes and next 5 ingredients. Cook 15 minutes or until desired consistency, stirring occasionally. Stir in shrimp, and simmer 5 minutes or until shrimp turn pink. Serve shrimp mixture over rice. Yield: 4 to 6 servings.

Creamy Shrimp Curry

6	cups water
2	pounds unpeeled medium-size fresh shrimp
½	cup minced onion
⅓	cup butter or margarine, melted
⅓	cup all-purpose flour
1	tablespoon curry powder
1	(14½-ounce) can ready-to-serve chicken broth
1½	cups milk
1½	teaspoons sugar
½	teaspoon salt
¼	teaspoon ground ginger
1	teaspoon lemon juice
	Hot cooked rice
	Assorted condiments

Bring water to a boil; add shrimp, and cook 3 to 5 minutes or until shrimp turn pink. Drain well; rinse with cold water. Peel and devein shrimp; set aside.

Cook onion in butter in a large skillet over medium-high heat, stirring constantly, until tender. Reduce heat to low; add flour and curry powder, stirring until smooth. Cook 1 minute, stirring constantly. Gradually add broth and milk; cook over medium heat, stirring constantly, until mixture is thickened. Stir in sugar, salt, ginger, and lemon juice. Add shrimp, and cook until heated.

Serve shrimp over rice with several of the following condiments: peanuts, sliced green onions, raisins, toasted coconut, and bacon pieces. Yield: 6 servings.

"Bubba Gump Shrimp became a household name. We had a whole bunch of boats—12 Jennys—a big old warehouse, and even our own hat that said Bubba Gump on it. And we made more money than Davy Crockett."

Shrimp Étouffée

2	pounds unpeeled medium-size fresh shrimp
3	cups water
2	cups chopped onion
4	cloves garlic, minced
2	tablespoons butter or margarine, melted
1	cup sliced green onions
3	tablespoons cornstarch
⅓	cup chopped fresh parsley
¾	teaspoon salt
¼	teaspoon ground white pepper
	Hot cooked rice

Peel and devein shrimp, reserving shells and tails. Chop shrimp, and set aside. Place shells and tails in a medium saucepan; add water, and bring to a boil. Cover, reduce heat, and simmer 30 minutes. Pour liquid through a wire-mesh strainer into a bowl, discarding shells and tails. Set strained stock aside.

    Cook chopped onion and garlic in butter in a large skillet over medium-high heat, stirring constantly, until tender. Add 2 cups of the reserved stock, and bring to a boil. Reduce heat to low; stir in shrimp and green onions. Cook 5 minutes, stirring occasionally.

    Combine cornstarch and an additional ½ cup reserved stock; gradually stir into shrimp mixture. Bring to a boil; boil, stirring constantly, 1 minute. Stir in parsley, salt, and pepper. Serve over rice. Yield: 8 servings.

"I happen to believe we make our own destiny. We have to do the best with what God gave us…"

you can
fry it

Crispy Sweet-and-Sour Shrimp

1½	pounds unpeeled medium-size fresh shrimp
½	cup all-purpose flour
¼	cup cornstarch
½	teaspoon baking powder
¼	teaspoon salt
½	cup water
1	teaspoon vegetable oil
1	large egg, lightly beaten
	Vegetable oil
	Hot cooked rice
	Sweet-and-Sour Sauce

Peel and devein shrimp; set aside. Combine flour and next 6 ingredients; stir until smooth. Pour oil to depth of 2 inches into a Dutch oven; heat to 375°. Dip shrimp into batter, and fry, a few at a time, until golden. Drain on paper towels. Serve over rice; top with sauce. Yield: 6 servings.

Sweet-and-Sour Sauce

½	cup sliced carrot
½	cup chopped green pepper
3½	tablespoons cornstarch
1	cup water, divided
½	cup sugar
½	cup white vinegar
⅓	cup catsup
1	tablespoon soy sauce
1	(15¼-ounce) can pineapple chunks, drained

Cook carrot in a small amount of boiling water 1 to 2 minutes; add green pepper, and cook an additional 1 minute. Drain and rinse with cold water. Set aside.

Combine cornstarch and ⅓ cup water, stirring until smooth. Combine remaining ⅔ cup water, sugar, and next 3 ingredients in a saucepan; bring to a boil over medium heat. Gradually stir cornstarch mixture into catsup mixture; cook, stirring constantly, until thickened. Stir in vegetable mixture and pineapple chunks. Yield: 3½ cups.

"Remember what I told you? Don't let anybody tell you they're better than you."

Coconut Fried Shrimp

½	pound unpeeled medium-size fresh shrimp
¾	cup pancake mix
¾	cup beer
	Vegetable oil
¼	cup all-purpose flour
1	cup flaked coconut

Peel shrimp, leaving tails intact; devein, if desired. Combine pancake mix and beer in a small bowl; stir until smooth.

Pour oil to depth of 2 inches into a Dutch oven; heat to 350°. Dredge shrimp in flour; shake off excess. Dip shrimp into batter; dredge in coconut. Fry, a few at a time, 45 seconds on each side or until golden. Drain on paper towels. Yield: 4 appetizer servings.

Fried Shrimp 'n' Apricot Sauce

1½	cups all-purpose flour
1	tablespoon paprika
1	teaspoon ground white pepper
½	teaspoon garlic powder
½	teaspoon dried Italian seasoning
1	(12-ounce) can beer
2	pounds unpeeled medium-size fresh shrimp
	Vegetable oil
	Apricot Sauce

Combine first 6 ingredients in a medium bowl; stir until smooth. Let batter stand 30 minutes.

Peel shrimp, leaving tails intact; devein, if desired. Pour oil to depth of 2 inches into a Dutch oven; heat to 375°. Dip shrimp into batter, and fry, a few at a time, until golden. Drain on paper towels. Serve with Apricot Sauce. Yield: 4 to 6 servings.

Apricot Sauce

1	cup apricot preserves
1	(4-ounce) jar diced pimiento, drained
2½	tablespoons white vinegar

Combine all ingredients in a saucepan. Bring to a boil over medium heat; reduce heat, and simmer 3 minutes, stirring occasionally. Cover and chill. Yield: 1⅓ cups.

"Well, destiny is when you're born to do something, but you don't know what it is."

Shrimp Scampi, page 86

Colorful Shrimp Stir-Fry, page 94

Walnut Fried Shrimp

16	unpeeled jumbo fresh shrimp
2	cups all-purpose flour
⅛	teaspoon salt
¼	teaspoon pepper
1	cup milk
2	large eggs, lightly beaten
2	cups ground walnuts
	Vegetable oil
	Commercial cocktail sauce
	Commercial tartar sauce

Garnishes: lemon wedges, fresh parsley sprigs

Peel shrimp, leaving tails intact; devein, if desired. Combine flour, salt, and pepper; stir well. Combine milk and eggs; stir well. Dip shrimp into egg mixture, and dredge in flour mixture. Dip shrimp into egg mixture again, and dredge in ground walnuts. Place coated shrimp on a wax paper-lined baking sheet; cover shrimp, and freeze 2 hours.

  Pour oil to depth of 2 to 3 inches into a Dutch oven; heat to 350°. Fry shrimp, a few at a time, until golden. Drain on paper towels.

  Arrange shrimp on a serving platter; serve with cocktail sauce and tartar sauce. Garnish, if desired. Yield: 4 servings.

Bubba's Beer-Batter Shrimp

1	pound unpeeled large fresh shrimp
¼	cup all-purpose flour
¼	cup cornstarch
⅛	teaspoon salt
¼	cup beer
2	tablespoons butter or margarine, melted
1	egg yolk
	Vegetable oil

Peel shrimp, leaving tails intact; devein, if desired. Combine flour, cornstarch, and salt. Add beer, butter, and egg yolk; stir until smooth.

　　Pour oil to depth of 2 inches into a Dutch oven; heat to 375°. Dip shrimp into batter; fry, a few at a time, until golden. Drain on paper towels. Yield: 2 to 4 servings.

Forrest's French-Fried Shrimp

2	pounds unpeeled medium-size fresh shrimp
1	cup all-purpose flour
1½	teaspoons baking powder
½	teaspoon salt
⅔	cup water
2	tablespoons lemon juice
1	tablespoon vegetable oil
1	large egg, lightly beaten
	Vegetable oil

Peel shrimp, leaving tails intact; devein, if desired. Combine flour, baking powder, and salt in a medium bowl. Add water and next 3 ingredients; stir until smooth.

Pour oil to depth of 2 inches into a Dutch oven; heat to 375°. Dip shrimp into batter, and fry, a few at a time, until golden. Drain on paper towels. Yield: 4 to 6 servings.

Gulf Coast Fried Shrimp

2	pounds unpeeled medium-size fresh shrimp
4	large eggs, beaten
⅔	cup commercial spicy French salad dressing
1½	tablespoons lemon juice
¾	teaspoon onion powder
	Vegetable oil
1⅓	cups crushed saltine crackers
⅔	cup crushed corn flakes cereal
⅓	cup white cornmeal

Peel shrimp, leaving tails intact; devein, if desired. Place shrimp in a large shallow dish. Combine eggs and next 3 ingredients; pour over shrimp, stirring gently. Cover and marinate in refrigerator 3 hours, stirring occasionally.

Pour oil to depth of 2 inches into a Dutch oven; heat to 375°. Combine cracker crumbs, cereal, and cornmeal. Remove shrimp from marinade, discarding marinade. Dredge shrimp in cracker mixture, and fry, a few at a time, until golden. Drain. Yield: 4 to 6 servings.

"I never really knew why she came back. Maybe it was Lt. Dan's thing... destiny... or maybe she just didn't have nowhere else to go. But I didn't care; it was like olden times."

Mama Blue's Shrimp Patties

3	cups water
1	pound unpeeled medium-size fresh shrimp
3	tablespoons butter or margarine
⅓	cup all-purpose flour
½	cup milk
2	green onions, chopped
1	teaspoon lemon juice
½	teaspoon Beau Monde seasoning
¼	teaspoon salt
¼	teaspoon pepper
¼	teaspoon paprika
¼	teaspoon hot sauce
1	large egg, lightly beaten
1	cup Italian-seasoned breadcrumbs, divided
¼	cup vegetable oil

"Sometimes I guess there just aren't enough rocks."

Bring water to a boil; add shrimp, and cook 3 to 5 minutes or until shrimp turn pink. Drain well; rinse with cold water. Chill. Peel, devein, and chop shrimp.

Melt butter in a heavy saucepan over low heat; add flour, stirring until smooth. Cook 1 minute, stirring constantly. Gradually add milk; cook over medium heat, stirring constantly, until mixture is thickened and bubbly. Stir in green onions and next 6 ingredients.

Combine shrimp, egg, ½ cup breadcrumbs, and sauce mixture. Shape into 4 patties; dredge in remaining crumbs. Pour oil to depth of ½ inch into a skillet. Fry in hot oil until golden, turning once. Drain. Yield: 4 servings.

you can
sauté it

Dilly of Some Shrimp

1¾	pounds unpeeled large fresh shrimp
2	tablespoons minced shallots
1	tablespoon minced garlic
2	tablespoons butter or margarine, melted
1	tablespoon olive oil
2	tablespoons lemon juice
1	tablespoon plus 1 teaspoon finely chopped fresh dill
⅛	teaspoon salt
⅛	teaspoon pepper

Garnishes: fresh dill sprigs, lemon slices

Peel and devein shrimp. Cook shallot and garlic in butter and olive oil in a large skillet over medium heat, stirring constantly, until tender. Stir in shrimp; cook 3 minutes or until shrimp turn pink, stirring occasionally. Stir in lemon juice and next 3 ingredients. Serve warm or cold. Garnish, if desired. Yield: 8 to 10 appetizer servings.

Shrimp Hot Brown

½	pound unpeeled medium-size fresh shrimp
2	tablespoons butter or margarine, melted
3	tablespoons butter or margarine
3	tablespoons all-purpose flour
1½	cups milk
1	packet instant broth and seasoning
1	teaspoon Old Bay seasoning
4	slices sandwich bread, toasted
½	cup (2 ounces) shredded Cheddar cheese
4	slices tomato
4	slices bacon, cooked and crumbled

Peel and devein shrimp. Cook shrimp in 2 tablespoons butter in a heavy saucepan over medium heat 5 minutes or until shrimp turn pink, stirring occasionally. Remove shrimp from saucepan, and set aside.

Melt 3 tablespoons butter in saucepan over low heat; add flour, stirring until smooth. Cook 1 minute, stirring constantly. Gradually add milk; cook over medium heat, stirring constantly, until mixture is thickened and bubbly. Stir in instant broth and Old Bay seasoning.

Place toast in an ungreased 11- x 7- x 2-inch baking dish; top evenly with shrimp. Spoon sauce over shrimp. Sprinkle evenly with cheese. Top each with a tomato slice. Bake, uncovered, at 450° for 12 to 15 minutes or until hot and bubbly. Sprinkle with bacon. Serve immediately. Yield: 4 servings.

"And we was like a family, Jenny and me. And it was the happiest time of my life... as close as you could get on this earth to God's heaven."

Shrimp Destin

2	pounds unpeeled large fresh shrimp
¼	cup chopped green onions
2	teaspoons minced garlic
1	cup butter or margarine, melted
1	tablespoon dry white wine
1	teaspoon lemon juice
⅛	teaspoon salt
⅛	teaspoon coarsely ground pepper
1	teaspoon dried dillweed
1	teaspoon chopped fresh parsley
2	French bread rolls, split lengthwise and toasted

Peel and devein shrimp. Cook green onions and garlic in butter in a large skillet over medium-high heat, stirring constantly, until tender. Add shrimp, wine, lemon juice, salt, and pepper; cook over medium heat 5 to 6 minutes or until shrimp turn pink, stirring occasionally. Stir in dillweed and parsley. Spoon shrimp mixture evenly over toasted rolls. Serve immediately. Yield: 4 servings.

Note: Shrimp Destin may be served over rice instead of rolls, if desired.

"I'm not a smart man, but I know what love is."

New Year's Steak 'n' Shrimp

6	unpeeled jumbo fresh shrimp
1	clove garlic, sliced
1	tablespoon butter or margarine, melted
3	tablespoons dry white wine
2	(1-inch-thick) beef tenderloin steaks

Garnish: fresh parsley sprigs

Peel and devein shrimp, leaving tails intact. Cook garlic in butter in a small skillet over medium heat, stirring constantly, 1 minute. Add shrimp; cook, stirring constantly, 5 minutes or until shrimp turn pink. Add wine; stir well. Cover mixture; set aside, and keep warm.

Place steaks on rack of a broiler pan; broil 5½ inches from heat (with electric oven door partially opened) 4 to 5 minutes on each side or to desired degree of doneness.

Place steaks on individual serving plates. Arrange shrimp on steaks; spoon wine sauce over shrimp. Garnish, if desired. Yield: 2 servings.

Shrimp Flambé (Hot Stuff!)

2	pounds unpeeled large fresh shrimp
1	tablespoon vegetable oil
2	tablespoons brandy
	White Wine Sauce
	Hollandaise Sauce

Peel and devein shrimp. Cook shrimp in hot oil in a large skillet over medium-high heat, stirring constantly, 3 to 5 minutes, or until shrimp turn pink. Drain. Reduce heat to low, and add brandy. Ignite with a long match when brandy is heated; stir until flames die down. Add White Wine Sauce and Hollandaise Sauce, stirring well. Serve immediately. Yield: 4 servings.

White Wine Sauce

¼	cup chopped onion
¼	cup chopped green pepper
2	cloves garlic, minced
1	tablespoon vegetable oil
1	tablespoon diced pimiento
2	tablespoons Chablis or other dry white wine
¼	teaspoon black pepper
	Dash of Worcestershire sauce
	Dash of hot sauce
2	tablespoons sour cream
1	tablespoon chopped fresh parsley

Cook first 3 ingredients in hot oil in a medium skillet over medium-high heat, stirring constantly, until crisp-tender. Stir in pimiento and next 4 ingredients; cover, reduce heat, and simmer 5 minutes, stirring occasionally. Stir in sour cream and parsley. Yield: ⅓ cup.

Hollandaise Sauce

3	egg yolks, beaten
⅛	teaspoon salt
	Dash of ground white pepper
2	tablespoons lemon juice
½	cup butter or margarine, divided

Combine egg yolks, salt, and pepper in top of a double boiler; gradually add lemon juice, stirring constantly. Add one-third of butter to egg mixture; cook over hot (not boiling) water, stirring constantly with a wire whisk, until butter melts. Add another one-third of butter, stirring constantly, until butter melts. As sauce thickens, stir in remaining one-third of butter. Cook, stirring constantly, until mixture is thickened. Yield: ¾ cup.

"They asked me if I was runnin' for women's rights... women are always right."

Shrimp Scampi

2	pounds unpeeled jumbo fresh shrimp
1	medium onion, finely chopped
4	cloves garlic, minced
½	cup butter or margarine, melted
2	tablespoons lemon juice
½	teaspoon dried tarragon
½	teaspoon steak sauce
½	teaspoon Worcestershire sauce
¼	teaspoon hot sauce
	Hot cooked fettuccine
2	tablespoons chopped fresh parsley

Peel and devein shrimp. Cook onion and garlic in butter in a large skillet over medium heat, stirring constantly, 4 minutes; add lemon juice and next 4 ingredients. Bring to a boil; add shrimp, and cook, stirring constantly, 3 to 5 minutes or until shrimp turn pink. Serve over fettuccine. Sprinkle with parsley. Yield: 4 to 6 servings.

"The sun, when it goes to bed, leaves little sparkles on the bayou…"

Angel Hair Pasta with Shrimp

8	unpeeled jumbo fresh shrimp
4	ounces angel hair pasta, uncooked
¼	cup olive oil
2	tablespoons minced garlic
1	teaspoon chopped shallots
6	spears fresh asparagus, cut into 2-inch pieces
½	cup sliced shiitake mushroom caps or ½ cup sliced fresh mushrooms
¼	cup peeled, seeded, and diced tomato
¼	teaspoon salt
⅛	teaspoon dried crushed red pepper
½	cup Chablis or other dry white wine
¼	cup freshly grated Parmesan cheese
1	tablespoon chopped fresh basil
1	tablespoon chopped fresh oregano
1	tablespoon chopped fresh thyme
1	tablespoon chopped fresh parsley

Peel and devein shrimp; set aside. Cook pasta according to package directions; drain and set aside.

Heat a 9-inch skillet over high heat 1 minute; add olive oil, and heat 10 seconds. Add shrimp, garlic, and shallot; cook, stirring constantly, 2 to 3 minutes or until shrimp turn pink.

Add asparagus and next 4 ingredients; stir in wine, scraping particles that cling to bottom of skillet, if necessary. Add pasta, Parmesan cheese, and remaining ingredients; toss gently. Serve immediately. Yield: 2 servings.

Shrimp and Feta Vermicelli

8	ounces vermicelli, uncooked
1	pound unpeeled medium-size fresh shrimp
	Pinch of sweet red pepper flakes
¼	cup olive oil, divided
⅔	cup crumbled feta cheese
½	teaspoon crushed garlic
1	(14½-ounce) can tomato wedges, undrained
¼	cup Chablis or other dry white wine
¾	teaspoon dried basil
½	teaspoon dried oregano
¼	teaspoon salt
¼	teaspoon pepper

Garnish: fresh basil sprigs

Cook vermicelli according to package directions; drain. Set aside, and keep warm.

Peel and devein shrimp. Cook shrimp and red pepper flakes in 2 tablespoons oil in a large skillet over medium heat, stirring constantly, 2 minutes or until shrimp turn slightly pink. Arrange in an ungreased 10- x 6- x 2-inch baking dish; sprinkle with cheese.

Add remaining oil to skillet; add garlic, and cook over low heat, stirring constantly, until tender. Add tomatoes; cook 1 minute. Stir in wine and next 4 ingredients; simmer, uncovered, 10 minutes, stirring occasionally. Spoon over shrimp. Bake, uncovered, at 400° for 10 minutes. Serve over pasta. Garnish, if desired. Yield: 3 servings.

Shrimp and Refried Rice

1	pound unpeeled medium-size fresh shrimp
2	tablespoons vegetable oil
¼	cup chopped onion
2	tablespoons chopped sweet red pepper
1	(8-ounce) can sliced water chestnuts, drained
1½	cups fresh broccoli flowerets
½	cup sliced fresh mushrooms
3	tablespoons soy sauce
1	large egg, lightly beaten
1½	cups cooked rice

Peel and devein shrimp; set aside. Pour oil around top of preheated wok or large skillet, coating sides; heat at medium-high (375°) for 2 minutes. Add onion and red pepper, and stir-fry 2 minutes. Add shrimp, water chestnuts, and next 3 ingredients; stir-fry 5 minutes.

Push shrimp mixture up sides of wok, forming a well in center. Pour egg into well, and stir-fry until set. Combine shrimp mixture and cooked egg. Add rice, and stir-fry 1 to 2 minutes or until thoroughly heated. Serve immediately. Yield: 4 servings.

"When the sun came up in the desert, Jenny, you couldn't tell where heaven ended and the earth started..."

Oriental Shrimp and Snow Peas

1	pound unpeeled medium-size fresh shrimp
½	teaspoon salt
1	teaspoon sesame or vegetable oil
1½	teaspoons cornstarch
¼	cup water
3	tablespoons oyster sauce
½	teaspoon cornstarch
¼	teaspoon chicken bouillon granules
¼	cup peanut or vegetable oil
2	teaspoons peeled, grated gingerroot
2	cloves garlic, crushed
½	pound fresh snow pea pods or 1 (6-ounce) package frozen snow pea pods, thawed
2	teaspoons rice wine or dry white wine

Peel and devein shrimp. Sprinkle shrimp with salt, and toss with sesame oil. Dredge shrimp in 1½ teaspoons cornstarch. Set aside. Combine water, oyster sauce, ½ teaspoon cornstarch, and bouillon granules; stir well. Set aside.

Pour peanut oil around top of preheated wok or large skillet, coating sides; heat at medium-high (375°) for 2 minutes. Add gingerroot and garlic, and stir-fry 30 seconds. Add shrimp, and stir-fry 3 to 5 minutes or until shrimp turn pink. Remove shrimp from wok, and drain on paper towels. Add snow peas to wok; stir-fry 30 seconds. Add cornstarch mixture to snow peas; stir-fry until slightly thickened. Stir in shrimp and wine. Serve immediately. Yield: 3 servings.

"If there's anything you need, Jenny, I won't be far away..."

"Mama always said, you got to put the past behind you before you can move on."

"I don't know if we all have a destiny, or if we're all just floatin' around accidental-like on a breeze."

Sizzlin' Szechuan Shrimp

2	pounds unpeeled medium-size fresh shrimp
½	cup water
½	cup catsup
¼	cup sugar
¼	cup chili sauce
2	tablespoons cornstarch
3	tablespoons dry sherry
1	tablespoon soy sauce
2	teaspoons sesame oil
¼	cup vegetable oil
6	green onions, chopped
3	cloves garlic, minced
1	(8-ounce) can water chestnuts, drained and chopped
1½	teaspoons dried crushed red pepper
1	teaspoon peeled, minced gingerroot
1	teaspoon cracked black pepper
	Hot cooked rice

Peel and devein shrimp; set aside. Combine water and next 7 ingredients; stir well, and set aside.

Pour vegetable oil around top of preheated wok or large skillet, coating sides; heat at medium-high (375°) for 2 minutes. Add green onions and next 5 ingredients; stir-fry 3 minutes. Add shrimp; stir-fry 3 minutes or until shrimp turn pink. Add catsup mixture, and cook 1 minute, stirring constantly, until thickened. Serve immediately over rice. Yield: 6 to 8 servings.

Colorful Shrimp Stir-Fry

1	pound unpeeled large fresh shrimp
½	teaspoon salt
½	teaspoon grated orange rind
¼	teaspoon dried crushed red pepper
1	teaspoon light sesame oil
½	pound fresh asparagus spears
⅓	cup chicken broth
3	tablespoons oyster sauce
1	tablespoon hoisin sauce
2	teaspoons cornstarch
3	tablespoons peanut oil
1	tablespoon minced garlic
1	tablespoon peeled, grated gingerroot
1	small sweet red pepper, cut into very thin strips
1	(7-ounce) jar baby corn, drained
2	teaspoons rice wine or dry white wine
	Hot cooked rice

Peel and devein shrimp. Place shrimp in a large bowl; sprinkle with salt, orange rind, and crushed red pepper. Add sesame oil, and toss gently to combine. Set aside.

    Snap off tough ends of asparagus. Remove scales from stalks with a knife or vegetable peeler, if desired. Cut asparagus diagonally into 1½-inch pieces. Set aside.

    Combine broth and next 3 ingredients; stir well, and set mixture aside.

    Pour peanut oil around top of preheated wok or large skillet, coating sides; heat at medium-high (375°) for

2 minutes. Add garlic and gingerroot, and stir-fry 30 seconds. Add shrimp mixture, and stir-fry 3 to 5 minutes or until shrimp turn pink. Remove shrimp from wok; drain on paper towels.

Add asparagus and sweet red pepper to wok, and stir-fry 1 minute or until tender. Remove from wok; set aside.

Add chicken broth mixture to wok; cook, stirring constantly, until thickened. Add shrimp, asparagus, sweet red pepper, baby corn, and wine to wok, and stir-fry just until thoroughly heated. Serve immediately over rice. Yield: 4 servings.

"Mama always said, God helps those who help themselves."

Tangy Honeyed Shrimp

1½	pounds unpeeled large fresh shrimp
3	tablespoons peanut oil
2	teaspoons minced garlic
1	teaspoon peeled, minced gingerroot
1	(10½-ounce) can condensed chicken broth, undiluted
1	tablespoon cornstarch
2	tablespoons honey
2	tablespoons catsup
1	tablespoon white vinegar
1	tablespoon rice wine or dry sherry
1	tablespoon soy sauce
⅛	teaspoon dried crushed red pepper
1	tablespoon sesame oil
1	teaspoon chopped fresh cilantro
2	green onions, cut into 1-inch pieces and shredded Rice Timbales

Garnish: fresh cilantro sprigs

Peel and devein shrimp. Pour peanut oil around top of a preheated wok or large skillet, coating sides; heat wok at high (400°) for about 1 minute. Add shrimp, garlic, and gingerroot, and stir-fry for 3 to 5 minutes or until shrimp turn pink.

 Combine chicken broth and next 7 ingredients, stirring until smooth. Add to shrimp mixture, stirring constantly. Bring to a boil; cook 1 minute. Stir in sesame oil, chopped

"I didn't have to think about money no more... which was good, I guess. One less thing."

cilantro, and green onions; cook until thoroughly heated. Serve immediately with Rice Timbales. Garnish, if desired. Yield: 3 to 4 servings.

Rice Timbales

2	cups water
½	teaspoon salt
1	cup long-grain rice, uncooked

Combine water and salt in a heavy saucepan; bring to a boil. Gradually add rice, stirring constantly. Cover, reduce heat, and simmer 20 to 25 minutes or until rice is tender and water is absorbed.

Press hot rice into 4 oiled 6-ounce custard cups. Immediately invert onto serving plates. Keep warm. Yield: 4 servings.

Creole Shrimp Jambalaya

1½	pounds unpeeled medium-size fresh shrimp
2	tablespoons vegetable oil
1	carrot, scraped and cut into thin strips
1	cup chopped onion
½	cup chopped green pepper
½	cup chopped celery
3	cloves garlic, minced
1	(14½-ounce) can whole tomatoes, undrained and chopped
1	(14½-ounce) can ready-to-serve chicken broth
1	(8-ounce) can tomato sauce
1¼	cups water
1	cup long-grain rice, uncooked
1	teaspoon salt
½	teaspoon dried thyme
½	teaspoon ground red pepper
¼	teaspoon chili powder
¼	teaspoon sugar
½	cup chopped fresh parsley
⅛	teaspoon hot sauce (optional)

Peel and devein shrimp. Cook shrimp in hot oil in a Dutch oven over medium heat, stirring constantly, 5 minutes or until shrimp turn pink. Remove shrimp with a slotted spoon; cover and chill.

Add carrot, onion, green pepper, celery, and garlic to Dutch oven; cook, stirring constantly, 3 minutes. Stir in tomatoes and next 9 ingredients. Bring mixture to a boil; cover, reduce heat, and simmer 45 minutes or until rice is tender and most of liquid is absorbed, stirring frequently. Stir in shrimp and parsley; simmer 10 minutes or until mixture is thoroughly heated. Add hot sauce, if desired. Yield: 4 servings.

> *"Now Mama said there's only so much money a man really needs, and the rest is just for showing off."*

Paella with Peas and Carrots

3	pounds chicken breasts, thighs, and legs
¼	cup olive oil
2	large onions, chopped
2	cloves garlic, minced
1	(28-ounce) can whole tomatoes, undrained and chopped
1	teaspoon salt
1	cup long-grain rice, uncooked
1	teaspoon dried oregano
½	teaspoon threads of saffron
¼	cup boiling water
1	(15-ounce) can soft-shelled or steamer clams in shell, drained, or 6 fresh cherrystone clams
1½	cups frozen English peas and carrots
2¼	pounds unpeeled medium-size fresh shrimp

"Jenny and I were like peas and carrots again."

Brown chicken in hot oil in a Dutch oven; remove chicken. Add onion and garlic to pan; cook over medium-high heat, stirring constantly, until tender. Add chicken, tomatoes, and salt. Cover and simmer 30 minutes.

Stir in rice and oregano. Dissolve saffron in boiling water; pour over chicken mixture. Cover and simmer 25 minutes. Add clams; cover and cook 10 minutes. Cook peas and carrots according to directions; drain. Peel and devein shrimp. Add shrimp to clam mixture; cover and cook 5 minutes or until shrimp turn pink. Spoon into center of serving dish. Spoon pea mixture around paella. Yield: 6 servings.

goes real good with

Old-Fashioned Sweet Coleslaw

1	small cabbage, finely chopped
2	carrots, shredded
⅓	cup mayonnaise or salad dressing
1	tablespoon sugar
½	teaspoon salt
¼	teaspoon pepper

Combine cabbage and carrot. Combine mayonnaise and remaining ingredients. Toss mayonnaise mixture with cabbage mixture. Cover and chill. Yield: 6 to 8 servings.

Sweet-and-Sour Hot Slaw

1	medium cabbage, shredded
¾	cup chopped onion
¾	cup chopped green pepper
1	cup sugar
1	cup white vinegar
1½	teaspoons salt
1	teaspoon celery seeds
1	teaspoon paprika
¾	teaspoon black pepper
½	teaspoon ground red pepper

Combine vegetables. Combine sugar and remaining ingredients; stir sugar mixture into vegetables. Cover and chill. Drain; spoon into a serving bowl. Yield: 8 to 10 servings.

"Shrimp is the fruit of the sea."

Bubba's Cocktail Sauce

1	cup chili sauce
⅓	cup lemon juice
3	tablespoons prepared horseradish
1	tablespoon Worcestershire sauce
¼	teaspoon hot sauce

Combine all ingredients; cover and chill. Yield: 1½ cups.

Delta Dunkin' Sauce

1	cup mayonnaise or salad dressing
2	tablespoons lemon juice
½	cup vegetable oil
¼	cup catsup
¼	cup chili sauce
1	teaspoon paprika
1	teaspoon pepper
1	teaspoon prepared mustard
1	teaspoon Worcestershire sauce
	Dash of hot sauce
2	cloves garlic, minced
1	small onion, grated

Combine all ingredients; cover and chill. Yield: 2¼ cups.

Finger Lickin' Rémoulade Sauce

1½	cups mayonnaise or salad dressing
2	hard-cooked egg yolks, sieved
2	tablespoons minced fresh parsley
2	cloves garlic, minced
1	tablespoon dried chervil
1	tablespoon paprika
1½	tablespoons Creole mustard
2	tablespoons white vinegar
1	tablespoon Worcestershire sauce
	Dash of hot sauce

Combine all ingredients; cover and chill. Yield: 1¾ cups.

Real Good Tartar Sauce

1	cup mayonnaise or salad dressing
¼	cup chopped dill pickle
1	tablespoon minced fresh parsley
2	teaspoons capers
2	teaspoons grated onion
1	teaspoon sugar
1	teaspoon prepared mustard
1	teaspoon lemon juice
¼	teaspoon garlic powder

Combine all ingredients; cover and chill. Yield: 1¼ cups.

Cracklin' Cornbread

2	cups cornmeal
2	teaspoons baking powder
1	teaspoon baking soda
¾	teaspoon salt
2	eggs, beaten
2	cups buttermilk
2	tablespoons vegetable oil
1	cup cracklings

Combine cornmeal, baking powder, soda, and salt in a large bowl; add eggs, buttermilk, oil, and cracklings, stirring just until dry ingredients are moistened.

Place a well-greased 10-inch cast-iron skillet in a 450° oven for 4 minutes or until hot. Remove from oven; spoon batter into skillet. Bake at 450° for 25 minutes or until lightly browned. Yield: 8 servings.

"Mama said, stupid is as stupid does."

Southern Hush Puppies

2	cups self-rising cornmeal
1	cup self-rising flour
½	teaspoon salt
3	tablespoons sugar
3	large eggs, lightly beaten
½	cup milk
1½	cups (6 ounces) shredded Cheddar cheese
2	jalapeño peppers, seeded and chopped
1	(17-ounce) can cream-style corn
1	large onion, chopped
	Vegetable oil

Combine first 4 ingredients in a large bowl. Combine eggs and milk; add to dry ingredients, stirring just until moistened. Stir in cheese, pepper, corn, and onion (do not overstir batter).

Pour oil to depth of 2 inches into a small Dutch oven; heat to 375°. Carefully drop batter by rounded tablespoons into oil; fry hush puppies, a few at a time, 3 minutes or until golden brown, turning once. Drain on paper towels. Yield: 3½ dozen.

"Bubba sure knew his shrimp."

Index

Accompaniments. *See also* Sauces.
  Coleslaw, Old-Fashioned Sweet, 102
  Cornbread, Cracklin', 105
  Hush Puppies, Southern, 106
  Slaw, Sweet-and-Sour Hot, 102
Appetizers
  Butter, Real Smooth Shrimp, 35
  Camouflage Shrimp-in-a-Pickle, 45
  Cheese Ball, Mighty Nice Shrimp, 39
  Cocktail, Bubba Gump's Shrimp, 41
  Coconut Fried Shrimp, 71
  Dilly of Some Shrimp, 80
  Dip, Spicy Shrimp, 34
  Jalapeño Cheese, Shrimp with, 42
  Layered Shrimp Appetizer, 40
  Lemon Shrimp, Lt. Dan's, 43
  Pizza Wedges, Shrimp, 23
  Quiches, Miniature Shrimp, 26
  Smiley Face Shrimp, 44
  Soufflé Roll, Feather, 46
  Spread, Zippy Shrimp, 36
  Stuffed Shrimp, Millionaire, 12
Baked
  Alabama-Style Shrimp Bake, 13
  Bayou la Batre Shrimp Mornay, 16
  Gruyère Cheesecake, Shrimp-, 24
  Jenny's Little Shrimp Casseroles, 18
  Mama's Shrimp Spaghetti, 21
  Noodle Bake, Shrimp and, 22
  Quiches, Miniature Shrimp, 26
  Quickie, Shrimp, 14
  Soufflé Roll, Feather, 46
  Stuffed Shrimp, Millionaire, 12
Barbecued
  Kabobs, Lemon-Garlic Shrimp, 28
  Kabobs, Shrimp and Vegetable, 32
  Lime-Barbecued Shrimp, 28
  Medal of Honor Shrimp Grill, 29
  Salad, Grilled Orange Shrimp, 30
  Southwestern Shrimp, Jenny's, 31
Boiled
  Bubba Gump's Shrimp Cocktail, 41
  Camouflage Shrimp-in-a-Pickle, 45
  Lt. Dan's Lemon Shrimp, 43
  Peas and Carrots, Shrimp with, 53
  Smiley Face Shrimp, 44
Broiled
  Beer-Broiled Shrimp, Bubba's, 15
  Dijonnaise, Shrimp, 14
  Stuffed Shrimp, Millionaire, 12
Cabbage, Slaws
  Old-Fashioned Sweet Coleslaw, 102
  Sweet-and-Sour Hot Slaw, 102
Casseroles
  Feta Vermicelli, Shrimp and, 88
  Jenny's Little Shrimp Casseroles, 18
  Mornay, Bayou la Batre Shrimp, 16
  Noodle Bake, Shrimp and, 22
  Spaghetti, Mama's Shrimp, 21
Cocktail
  Bubba Gump's Shrimp Cocktail, 41
  Sauce, Bubba's Cocktail, 103
Cornbreads
  Cracklin' Cornbread, 105
  Hush Puppies, Southern, 106
Creole
  Four-Square Gospel Creole, 66
  Jambalaya, Creole Shrimp, 98
Curry, Creamy Shrimp, 67
Etouffée, Shrimp, 68
Fried
  Beer-Batter Shrimp, Bubba's, 76
  Coconut Fried Shrimp, 71
  Crispy Sweet-and-Sour Shrimp, 70

Forrest's French-Fried Shrimp, 76
Fried Shrimp 'n' Apricot Sauce, 72
Gulf Coast Fried Shrimp, 77
Mama Blue's Shrimp Patties, 78
Walnut Fried Shrimp, 75

Gumbos
　Chicken Gumbo, Shrimp 'n', 58
　Greenbow County Okra Gumbo, 60

Hush Puppies, Southern, 106

Jambalaya, Creole Shrimp, 98

Kabobs
　Lemon-Garlic Shrimp Kabobs, 28
　Vegetable Kabobs, Shrimp and, 32

Mornay, Bayou la Batre Shrimp, 16

Omelet, Shrimp and Cheese, 64

Paella with Peas and Carrots, 100

Pasta
　Angel Hair Pasta with Shrimp, 87
　Noodle Bake, Shrimp and, 22
　Spaghetti, Mama's Shrimp, 21
　Vermicelli, Shrimp and Feta, 88

Quiches, Miniature Shrimp, 26

Salads
　Bean Salad, Caribbean Shrimp-, 52
　Gulf Shrimp and Vegetables, 65
　Mama's Best Shrimp Louis, 49
　Mrs. Blue's Shrimp Salad, 50
　Orange Shrimp Salad, Grilled, 30
　Oriental Shrimp Salad, 51
　Peas and Carrots, Shrimp with, 53
　Uptown Shrimp Salad, 48

Sandwich
　Shrimp Hot Brown, 81

Sauces
　Apricot Sauce, 72
　Cocktail Sauce, Bubba's, 103
　Dunkin' Sauce, Delta, 103
　Hollandaise Sauce, 85
　Rémoulade Sauce, Finger Lickin', 104
　Sweet-and-Sour Sauce, 70
　Tartar Sauce, Real Good, 104
　Tomato Sauce, Italian, 25
　Wine Sauce, White, 84

Sautéed
　Angel Hair Pasta with Shrimp, 87
　Creole Shrimp Jambalaya, 98
　Destin, Shrimp, 82
　Dilly of Some Shrimp, 80
　Feta Vermicelli, Shrimp and, 88
　Flambé, Shrimp, 84
　Oriental Shrimp and Snow Peas, 90
　Paella with Peas and Carrots, 100
　Refried Rice, Shrimp and, 89
　Scampi, Shrimp, 86
　Steak 'n' Shrimp, New Year's, 83
　Szechuan, Sizzlin' Shrimp, 93

Scampi, Shrimp, 86

Soufflé Roll, Feather, 46

Soups
　Chowder, Route 19 Shrimp, 54
　Enchilada Soup, Tex's Shrimp, 62
　Gazpacho, Peace March Shrimp, 57
　Gumbo, Greenbow County Okra, 60
　Gumbo, Shrimp 'n' Chicken, 58
　Stock, Old Reliable Shrimp, 63

Steamed Shrimp, Mama Blue's, 8

Stuffed Shrimp, Millionaire, 12

Sweet-and-Sour Shrimp, Crispy, 70

… shrimp flambé, shrim[p
]shrimp spread, shrimp j[
]shrimp soup, beer-broil[ed
]shrimp, shrimp mornay[,
]shrimp cheesecake, shri[mp
]shrimp, sherried shrimp[,
]rolled shrimp soufflé, sh[rimp
]carrots, shrimp gazpach[o,
]beer-batter shrimp, shri[mp
]shrimp. That's… that's a[